CELTIC ART

'The work, not of men, but angels.'

Description of the *Book of Kells* by the

13th century historian Giraldus Camrensis

CELTIC ART

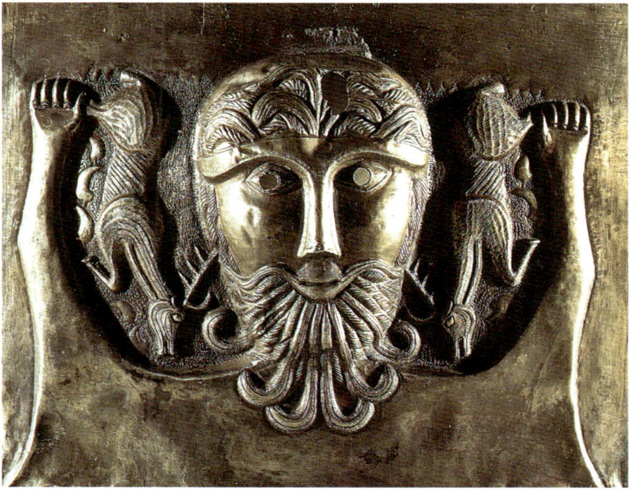

BROCKHAMPTON PRESS
LONDON

TITLE PAGE

GUNDESTRUP CAULDRON,

- HEAD OF CERNUNNOS

Detail from the Gundestrup Cauldron of the head of Cernunnos, the deer-god. The cauldron is made of silver gilt plates, with gold plating, each part created by several different craftsmen.

CELTIC CIVILISATION occupied the centre stage of much of Continental Europe, as well as the British Isles from as early as 700BC. After 100AD, the culture of the Celts became intermingled with that of the aggressors who overran the tribes: Romans, Angles, Saxons, Vikings, Normans and Huns. However, in parts of Wales, the Western Isles of Scotland, and most significantly in Ireland, Celtic artistic traditions remained unshaken.

There was no such thing as a typical Celt; customs and culture differed from tribe to tribe and from region to region, as well as evolving over time, from the early pagans until the establishment of Christianity, therefore making it impossible to give a general description of a unified artistic style.

If there can be said to be a consistent theme running through the art of the Celts, it would be nature and the natural. Until Christianity offered them one God, Celtic deities were many and varied but principally concerned with herd and harvest. Art was basically decorative, and cannot be separated from the religion and magic that underlie many of the most typical motifs. Such sacred symbols as the human head, the heads of venerated birds and beasts, trees and flowers were used to decorate weapons and jewellery, as well as pots, vases and mysterious votive objects, whose function is unknown.

This mythical, abstract art of a pagan world might seem irreconcilable with the teaching of Christianity; but in the illuminated manuscripts of the monasteries off the West of Scotland and the Northumbrian coast, inspiration was drawn from "barbarian" Celtic patterns, rather than from Roman and Late Antique styles. In the Book of Kells, angels are depicted in a tangled mass of Celtic knotwork with animals such as otters, salmon, cats and hares, demonstrating that all creatures which had been of mystic importance to pagan Celts, were equally significant in God's kingdom.

The art of the Celts always fulfiled a purpose, whether it was to impress neighbouring tribes when covering weapons and jewellery, or to convey holiness in Christian illuminated manuscripts. Never far away was the sense of the natural world, manifesting itself in the curling vine tendrils, and strange beasts and fish appearing from tangled foliage, which was omnipresent and all-important in the Celtic world. The rich colours, intricate patterns and bold sculptures of this extraordinary collection is the brilliant artistic legacy of the Celts.

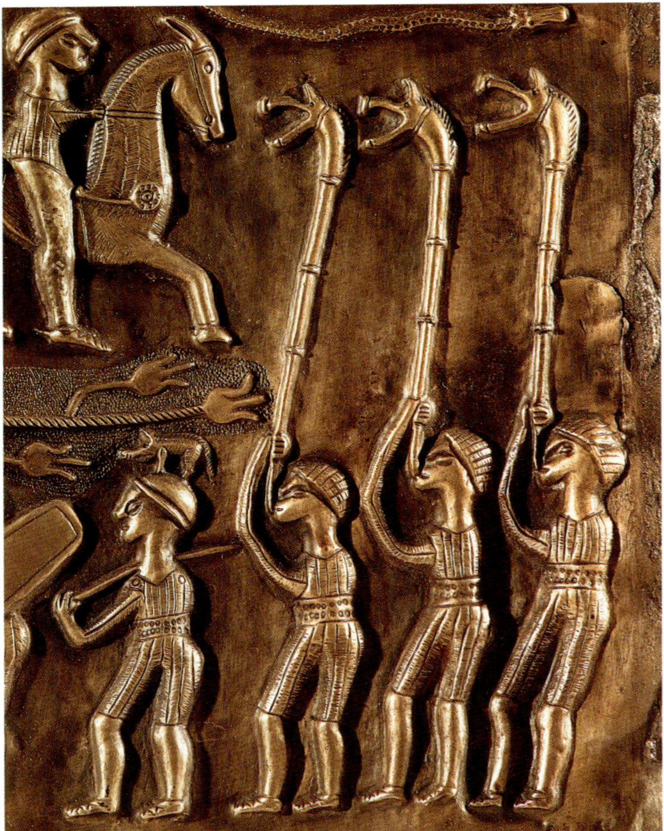

Relief from the Gundestrup Cauldron *left*

Detail from the Gundestrup Cauldron, found in a moor near Gundestrup, Jutland in 1891, and dating from the 1st century BC. Cauldrons were probably produced for ritual purposes; this relief shows a ceremonial procession with carnyx (lur) players in honour of Cernunnos, the deer-god.

Detail from the Gundestrup Cauldron - man on dolphin

overleaf Relief from the Gundestrup Cauldron showing a man riding on a dolphin, pursued by a boar: probably an incident from Celtic mythology.

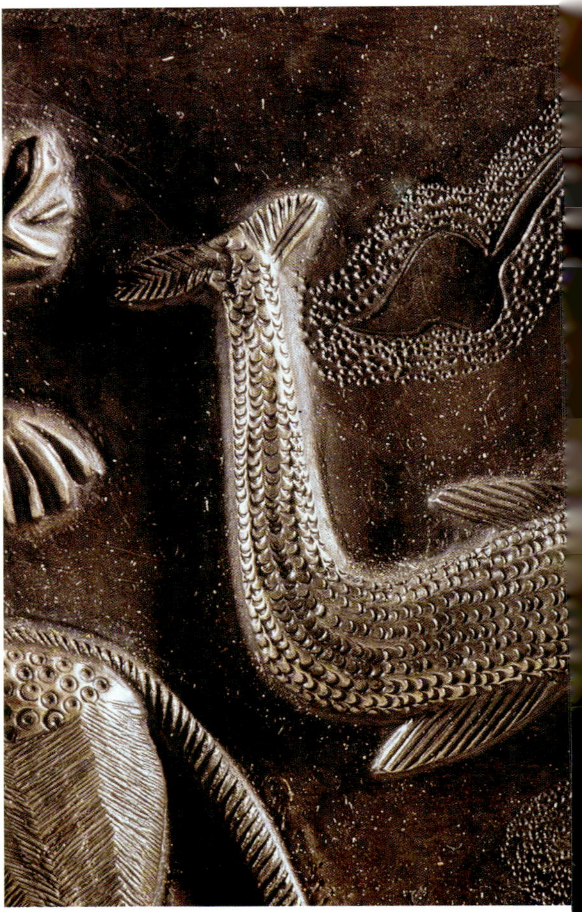

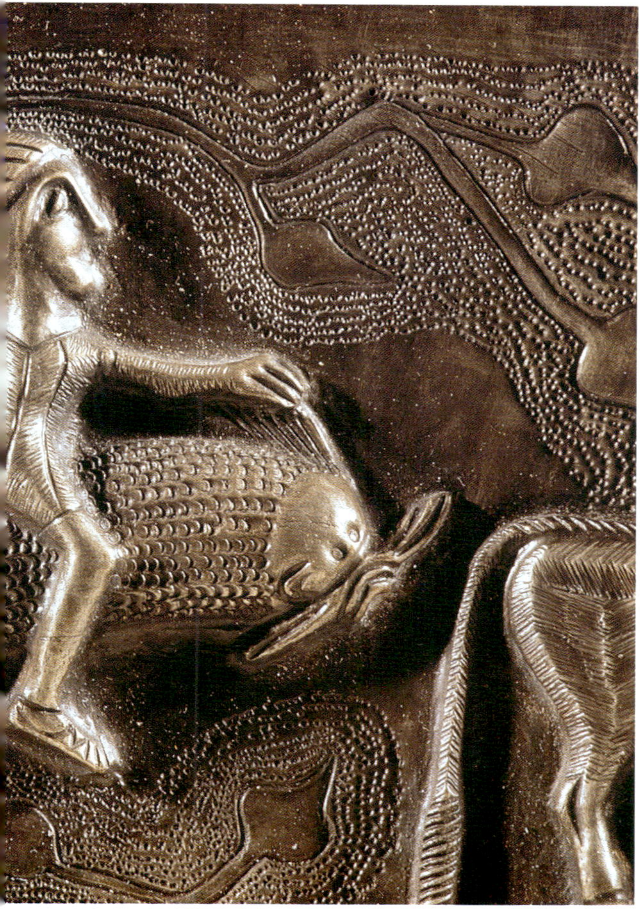

EARLY CELTIC HELMET *right*

This ceremonial helmet was found in Amfreville-sous-les-Monts, France, and dates from the late 4th century BC. It is made of bronze, and decorated with gold, iron and enamel; the foliage pattern shows a strong northern Italian influence, as it was about this time that Celtic tribes began their most intense period of expansion southwards and eastwards into Europe.

SCULPTURES - HUMAN HEADS AND BIRD'S BEAK

overleaf Sculpture of twin heads, separated by a bird's beak; 4th century BC. Unearthed in a temple at Roquepertuse, France, these heads could refer to the Celtic gods with two faces, who had the power to look ahead to the next world and, at the same time, to the living world of men.

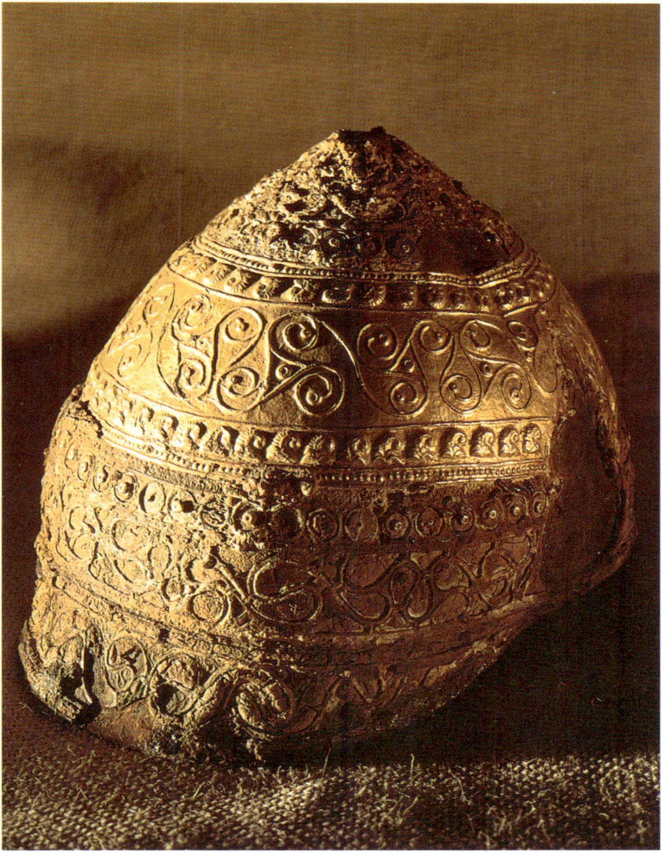

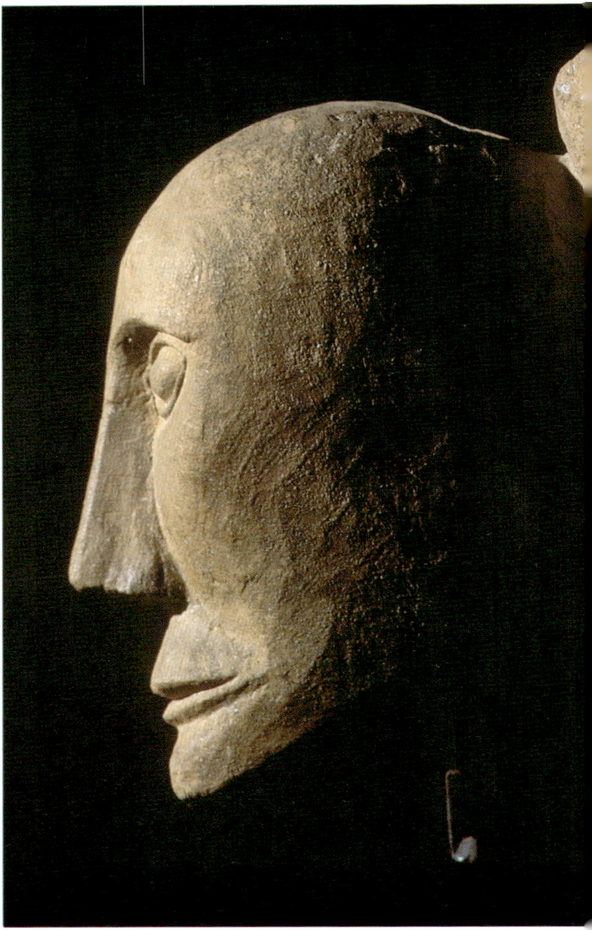

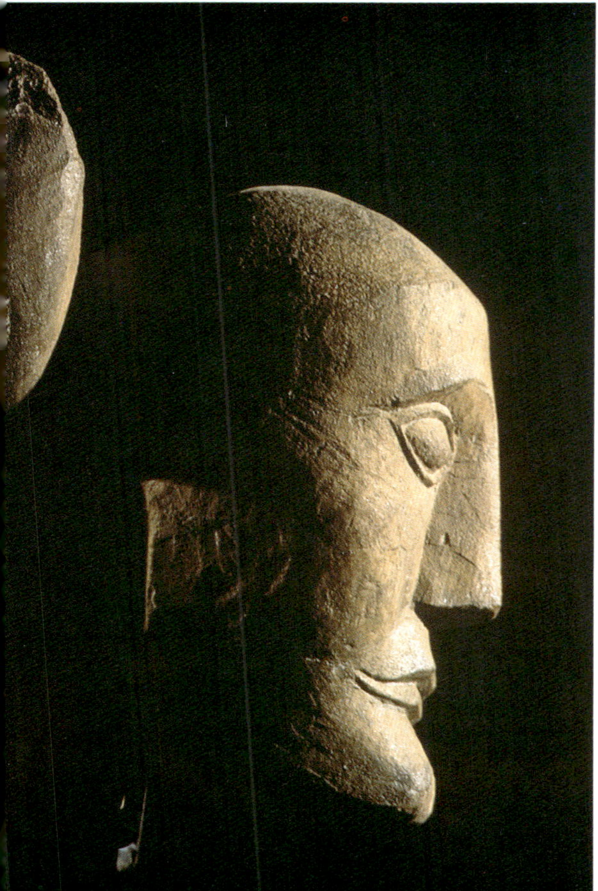

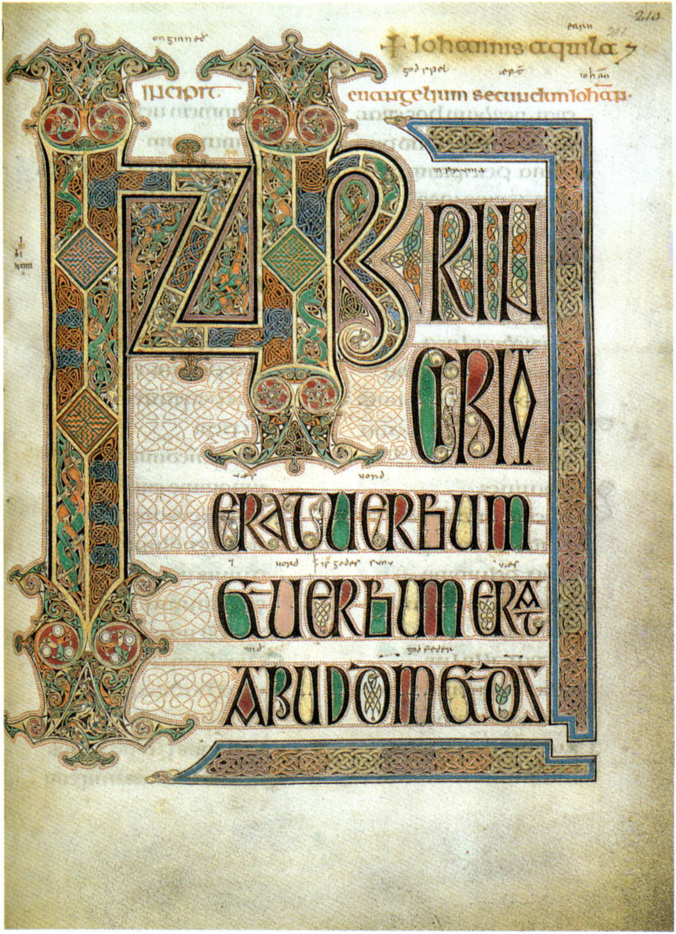
Iohannis aquila
Incipit evangelium secundum Iohan.
RIN
CIPIO
ERAT UERBUM
ET UERBUM ERAT

BEGINNING OF ST. JOHN'S GOSPEL

left The initial page of St. John's Gospel; taken from the Lindisfarne Gospels, illuminated by Eadfrith, Bishop of Lindisfarne, Northumbria in 698. An inscription in the manuscript tells us that 'Eadfrith originally wrote this book for God and St. Cuthbert.' The painstaking detail required great discipline and was seen as another way of praising God.

Cross - carpet page, Lindisfarne Gospels

right One of the five paintings in the Lindisfarne Gospels known as carpet pages. This design, which introduces the gospel of St. John, incorporates the Christian cross into an intricate bed of Celtic knotwork and intertwining birds.

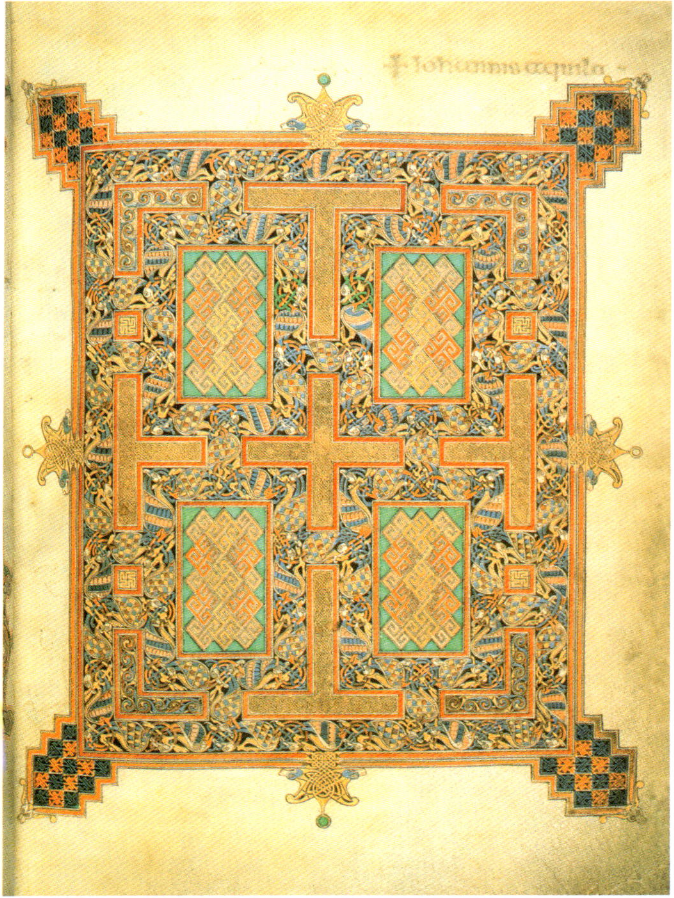
Iohannis aquila

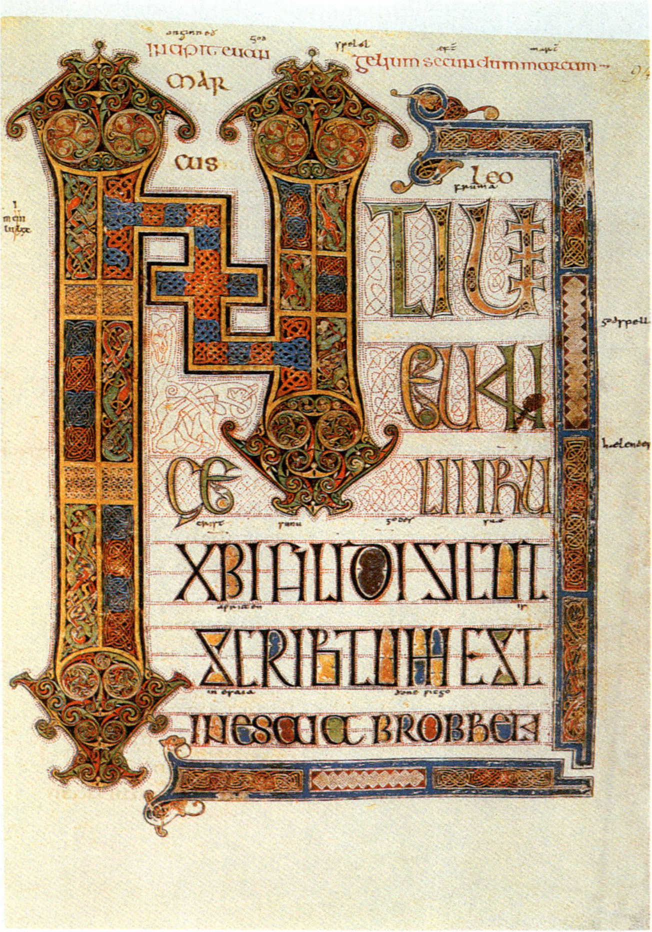
Mar
cus
leo
94

St. Mark's Gospel

left Initial page of the Gospel of St. Mark, Lindisfarne Gospels. Each gospel was illuminated on vellum (parchment made from animal skin). The reddish-brown hair remaining on the manuscripts suggests that this vellum was made from cattle rather than sheep.

Bird of prey *right*

Stone sculpture of a bird of prey, dating from the 4th-3rd century BC, found in the Sanctuary of Roquepertuse in France. Many birds were symbols of divinity for the Celts.

Sculpture - chariot with animals *overleaf*

Bronze sculpture of a Celtic nobleman hunting a boar, dating from as early as the 5th century BC, and found in Merida, Spain. The tableau is set on a movable wagon with bells that tinkle; the sculpture might represent a Celtic deity or could have been a sophisticated toy.

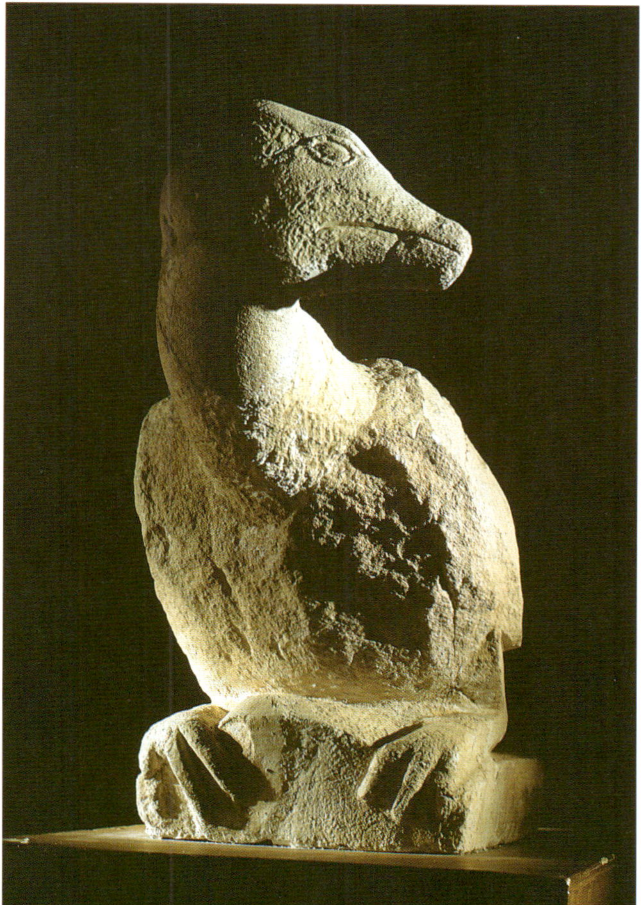

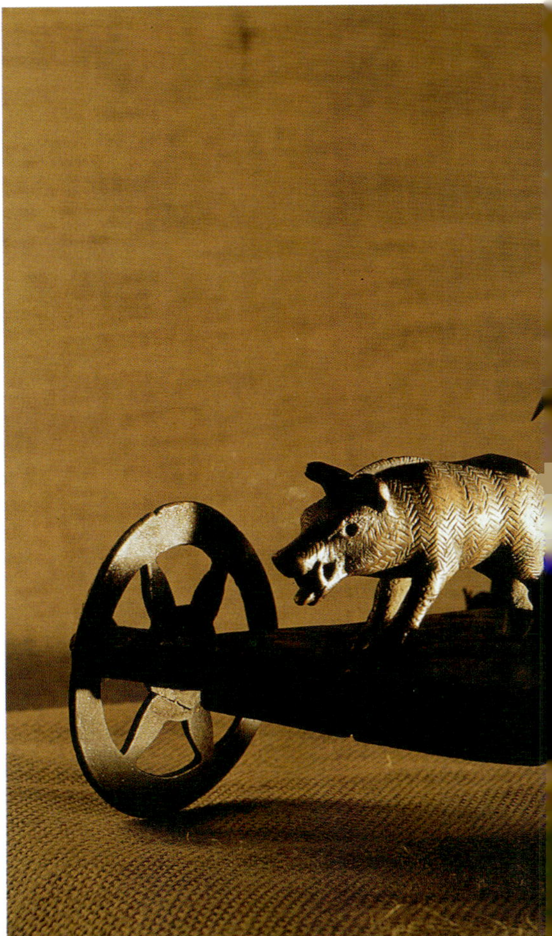

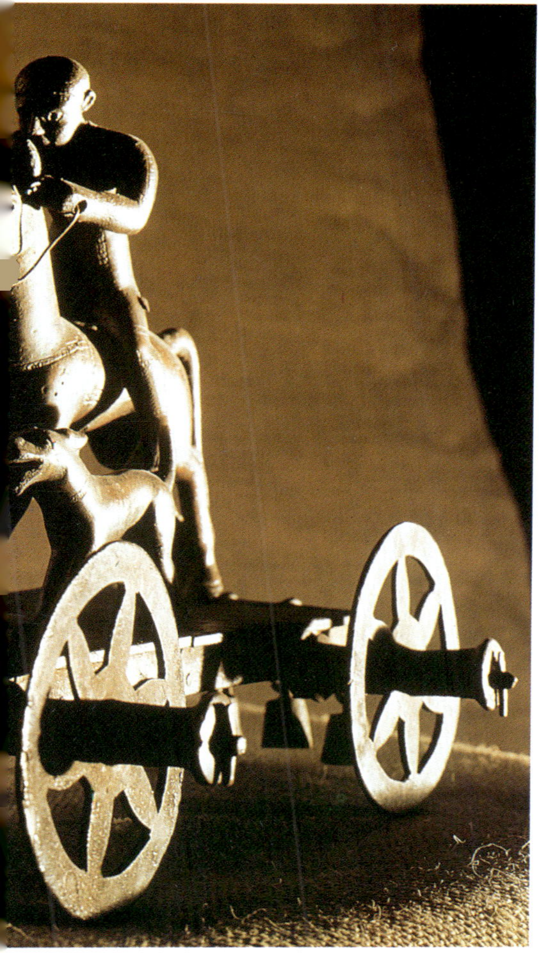

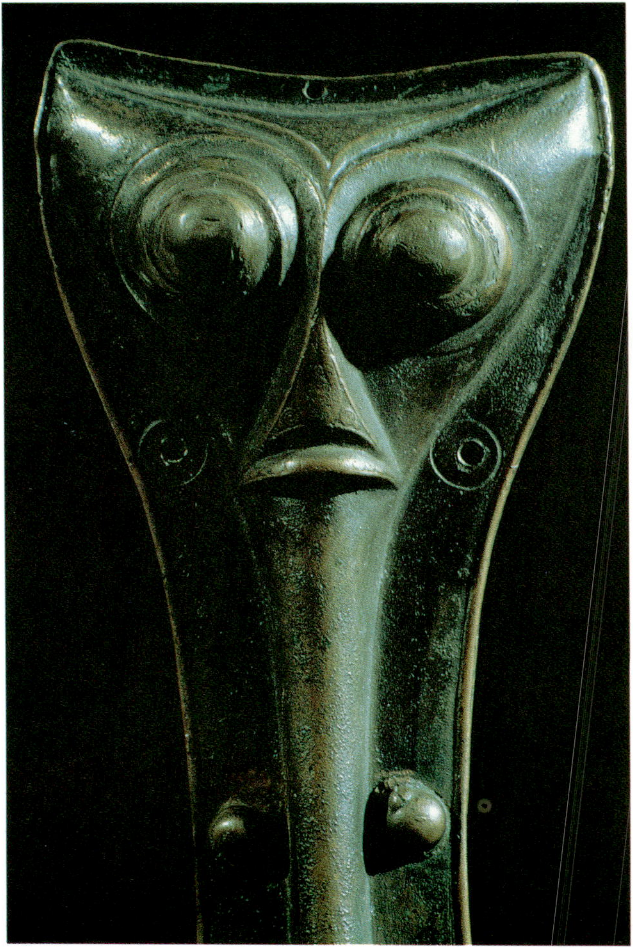

WEAPONS - DETAIL OF A BRONZE SHIELD *left*
Detail of a bronze shield, found in the Thames near Wandsworth, and dating from the 3rd century BC. The more the Celts prospered, the more they occupied themselves with warfare; thus blacksmiths were constantly encouraged to outdo themselves in the production of ever more impressive weapons with which to intimidate their enemies.

METALWORKS - ENAMELLED HORSE'S HARNESS *overleaf* Enamelled decorative harness mount, possibly dating from the 1st century AD. The mount could be attached to a strap and used to dress up a chariot horse.

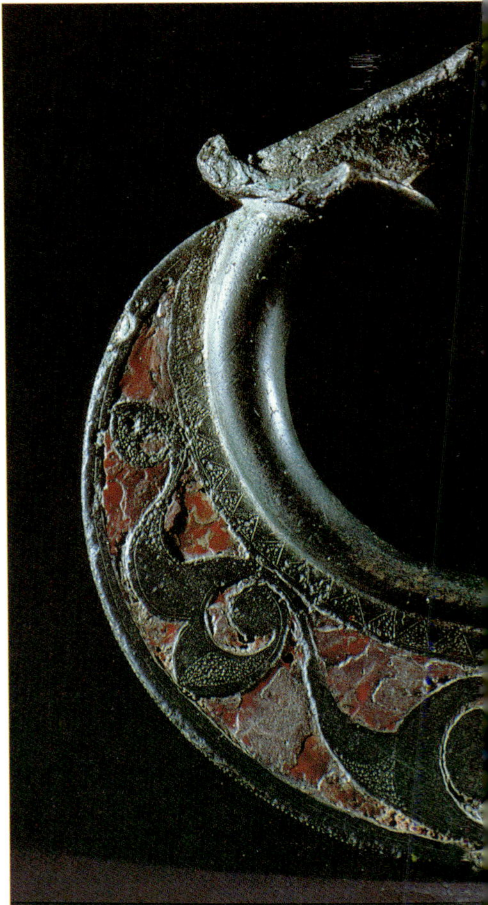

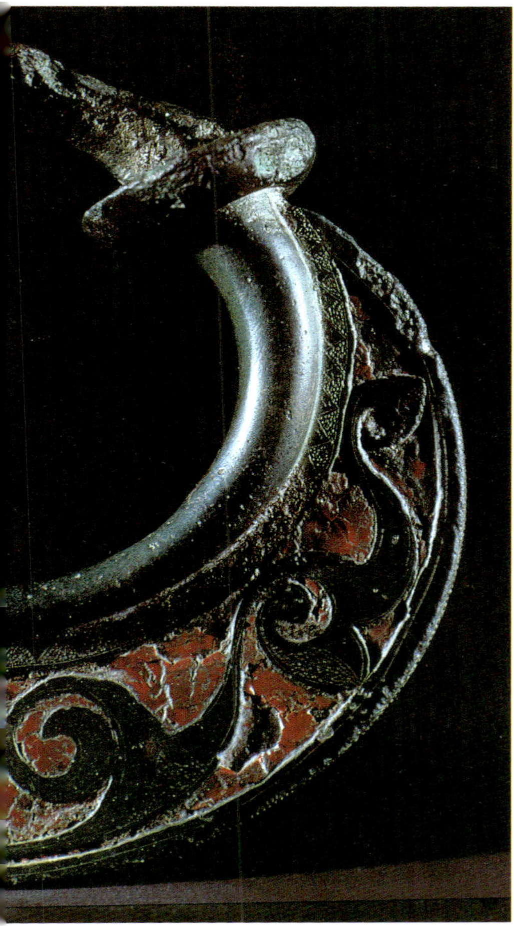

BRONZE JUG DECORATION *right*

Part of the bronze decoration on a wooden jug, found in Brno-Malomerice in former Czechoslovakia, and dating from the 3rd century BC. Julius Caesar said of the Celts that they were 'exceedingly given to religious superstition': the strange face on this jug may well have been intended to ward off evil and invite the protection of friendly spirits.

SCULPTURE - WATERBIRD JUG *overleaf*

The spout of a bronze jug, fashioned in the shape of a water bird; found in the Moselle region of France, and dating from the 4th century BC. Water birds (such as ducks, geese and swans) represented certain gods and goddesses; the swan stood for purity and was used as a disguise by gods who wanted to pursue innocent maidens.

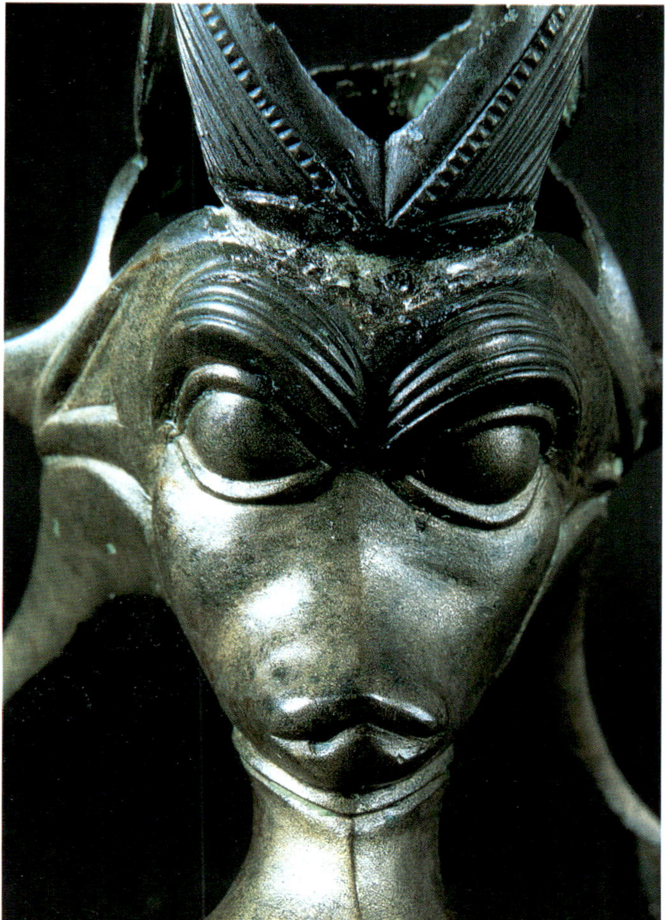

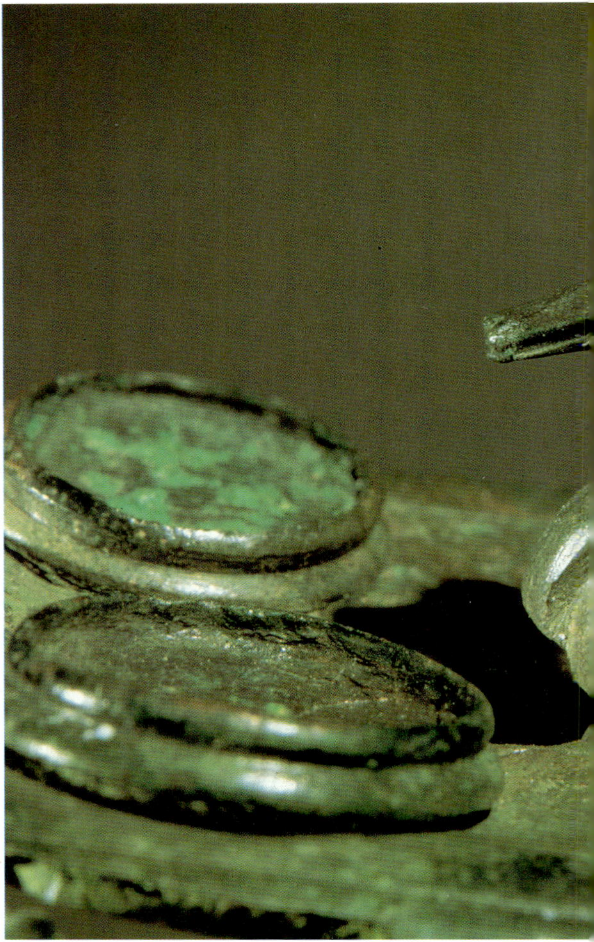

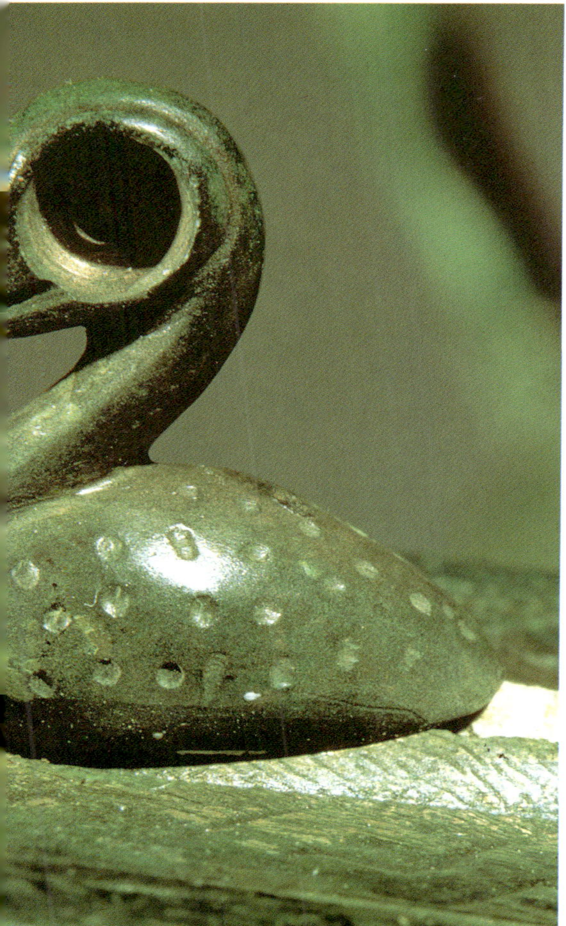

SCULPTURE - STATUETTE OF HORSE WITH HUMAN HEAD

right Statuette of a horse with a human head from the 5th century BC; found in the tomb of a Prince in Reinheim, Germany. Legends of the Centaurs (half-men and half-horse) originated in Ancient Greece.

GOLDSMITHERY - GOLD NECK COLLAR *overleaf*

Gold neck collar, dating from the mid-4th century BC. Such necklaces, or 'torques', were among the most characteristic ornaments worn by the Celts, indicating the social and religious status of the wearer.

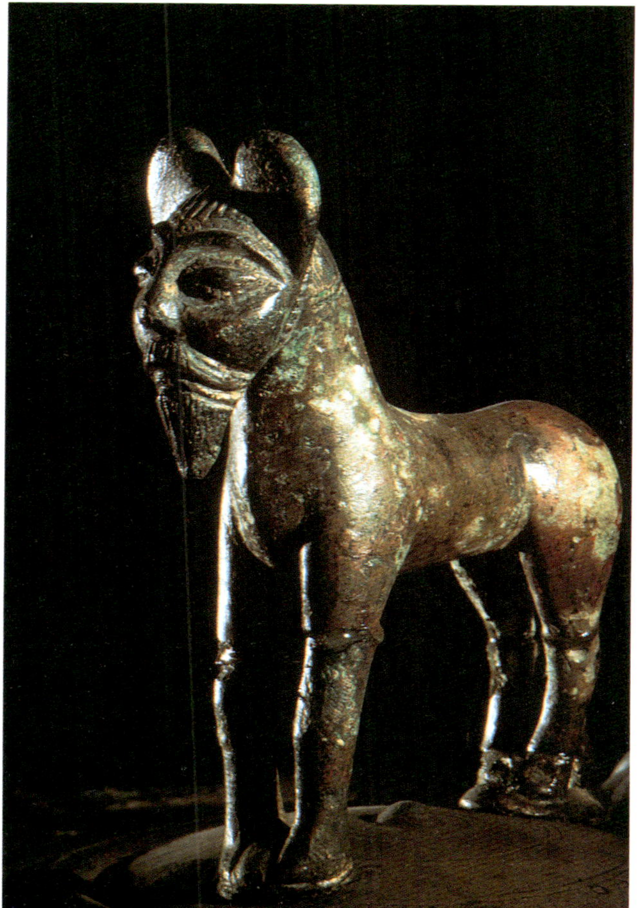

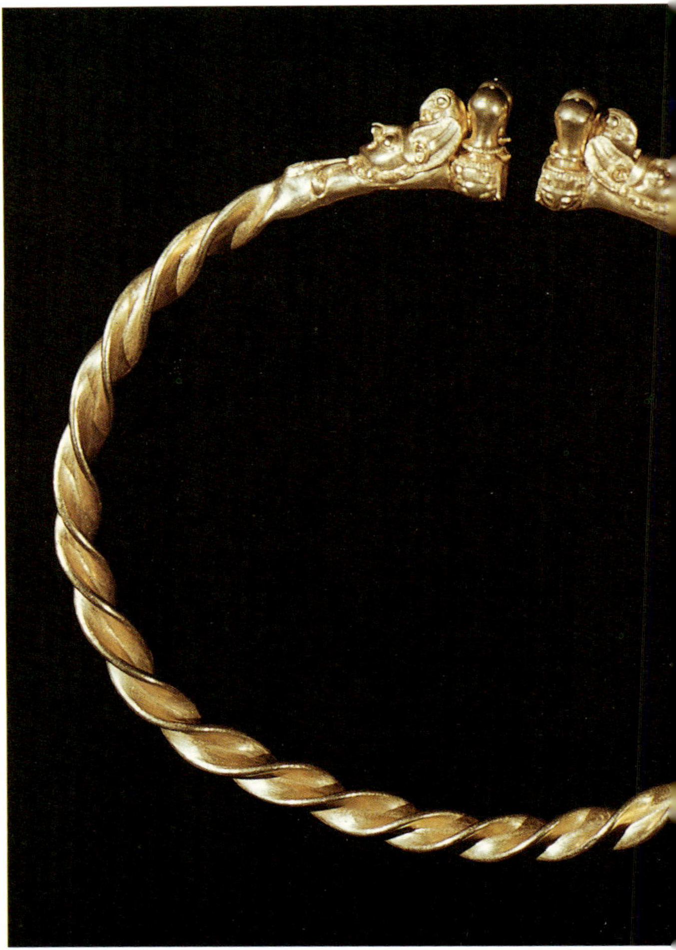

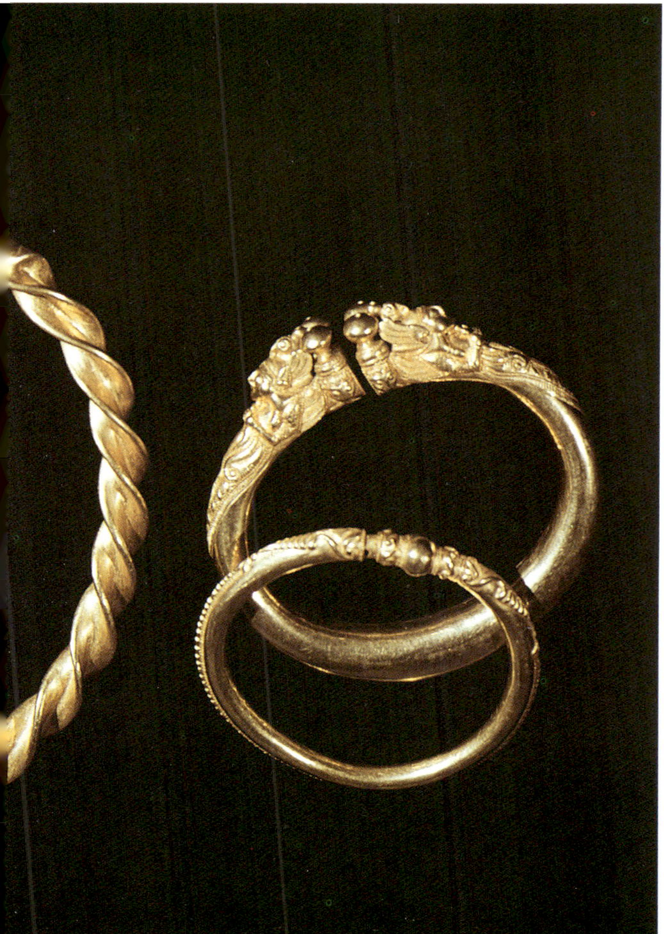

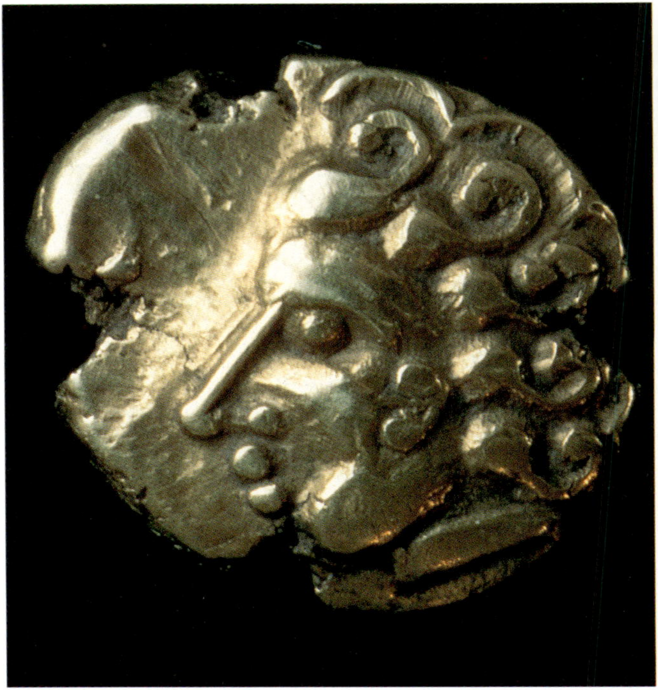

Celtic coin *left*

Celtic coin from the minting area of the Volcae, found in the Black Forest; dating from the second half of the 2nd century BC. The head pictured is probably that of a Celtic chief.

PLATE OF HORSE'S ARMOUR *right*

Open-worked bronze plate of horse's armour, found in London, and dating from the 1st century BC. Such an elaborate adornment was probably intended for a ceremonial parade, rather than for use in battle.

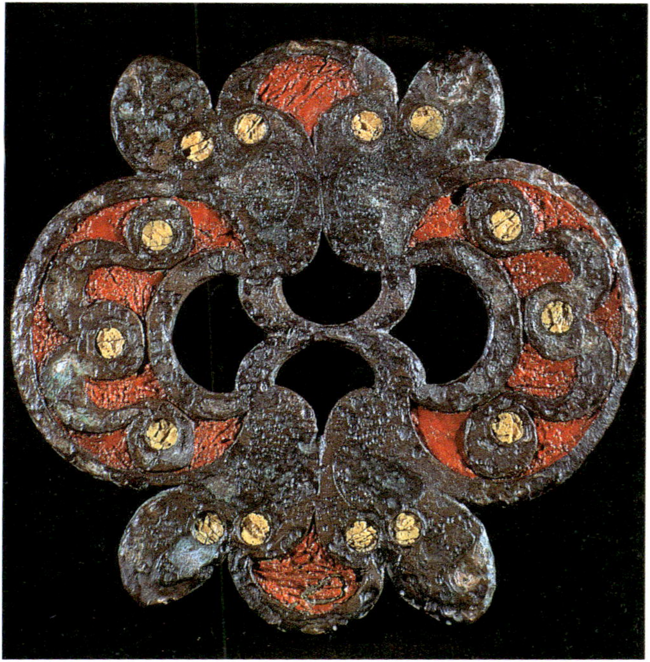

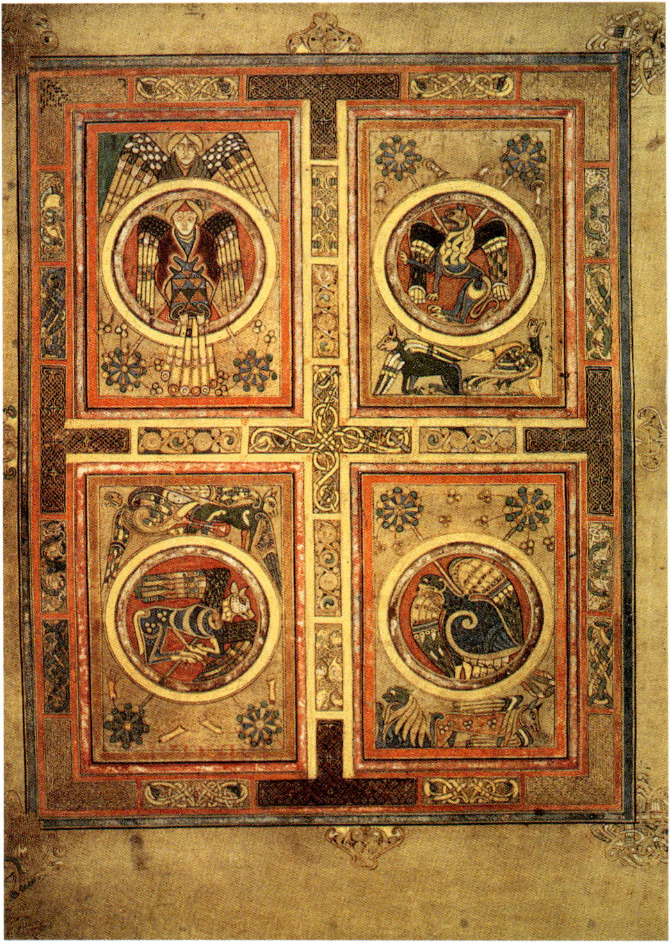

Book of Kells - symbols of the four evangelists

left Page from the Book of Kells showing the symbols of the four evangelists, which were winged figures with the appearance of a man, a lion, a calf and an eagle. St. Gregory explained these symbols as the four stages of Christ's life: representing birth, death, resurrection and ascension.

Book of Kells - symbols of the four evangelists

right Page from the Book of Kells showing the symbols of the Four Evangelists. The Book of Kells was probably made on the island of Iona on the west Scottish coast, shortly before the island was sacked by the Vikings in 807.

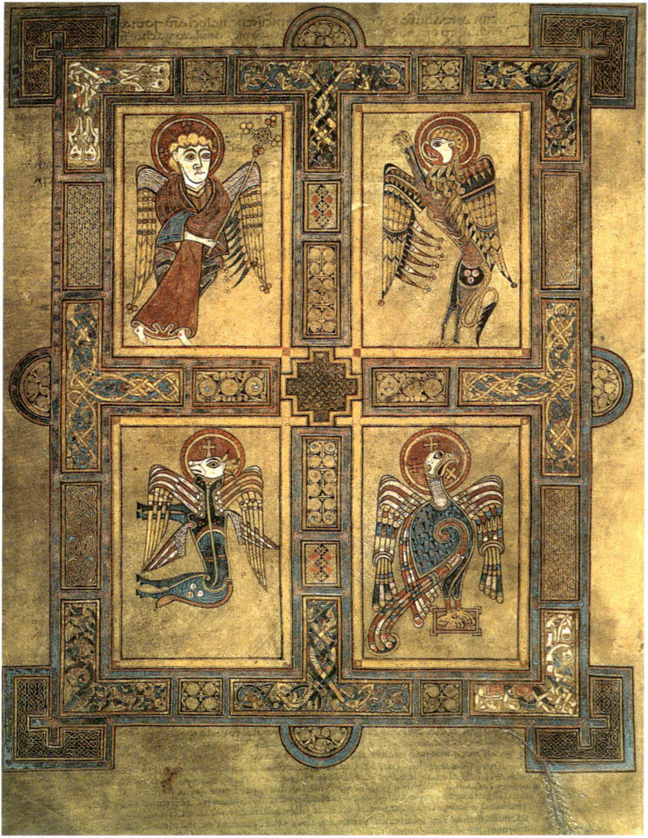

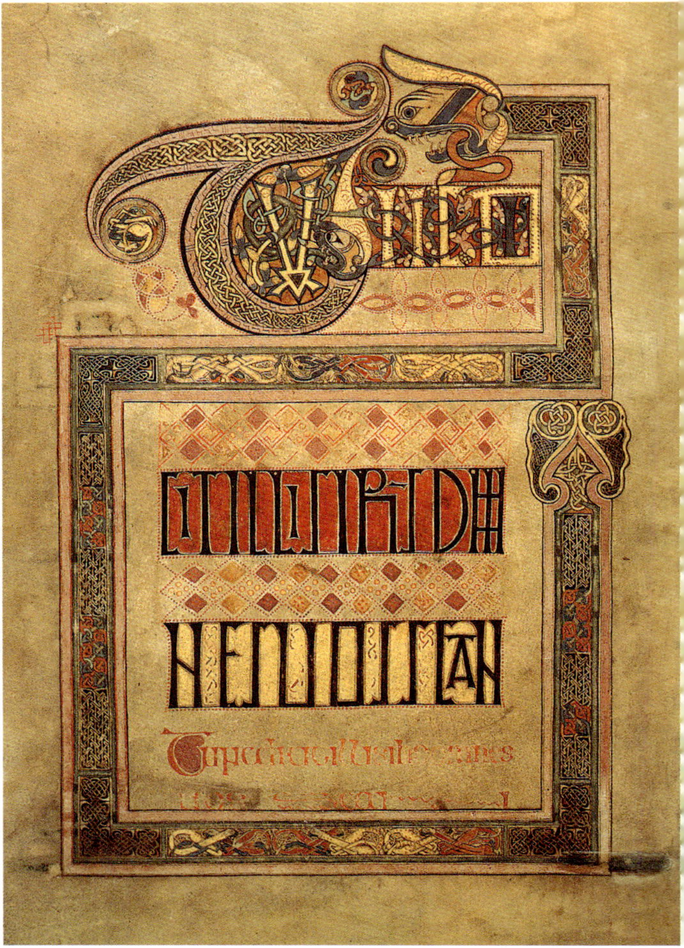

Book of Kells - 'Tunc dicit.'

left Initial page from the Book of Kells. Interwoven with the Celtic knot designs are various beasts and plants: the shamrock at the bottom left corner of the main 'T' initial could represent St. Patrick, the saint who allegedly brought Christianity to Ireland.

Metalworks - human head bucket handle *right*

Bronze human head capped with a crested helmet, on the handle of the bronze reinforcement of a wooden bucket. Found in a 1st century BC grave in Aylesford, Kent, the bucket was probably used as a cremation urn.

Early sculpture - two severed heads *overleaf*

Sculpture of two heads of decapitated bodies, found near Aix-en-Provence, France, and dating from as early as the 3rd century BC. The Celts believed that a human head could remain alive after the death of the body and that a severed head could stave off evil and bring good luck.

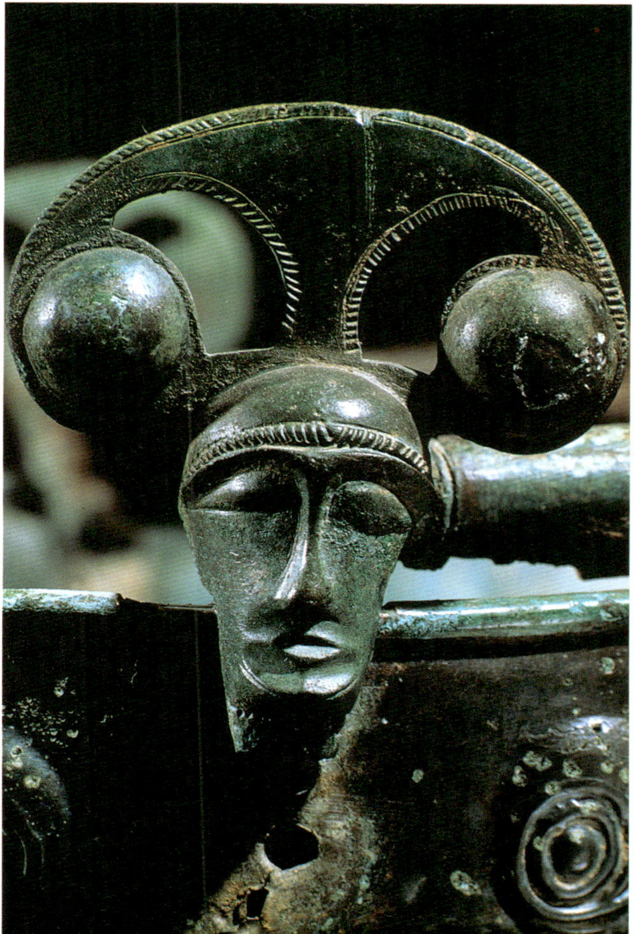

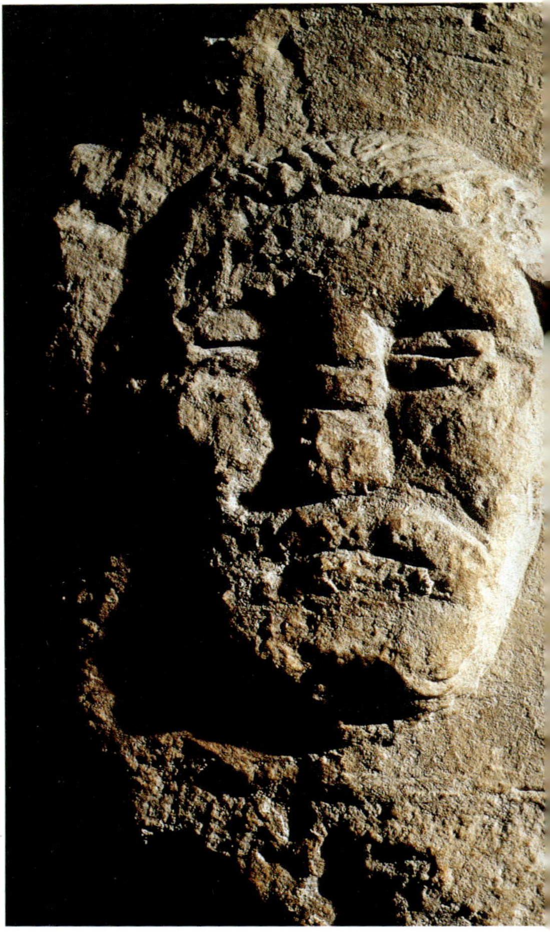

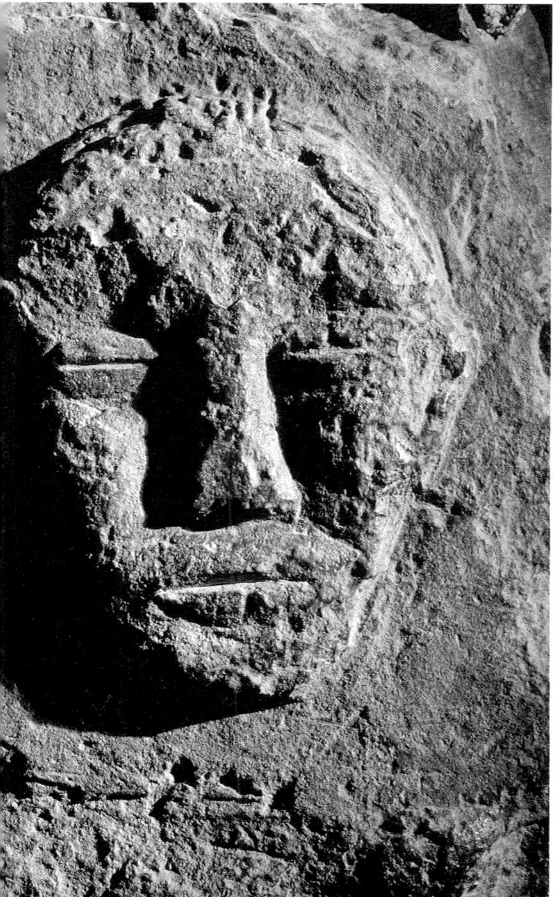

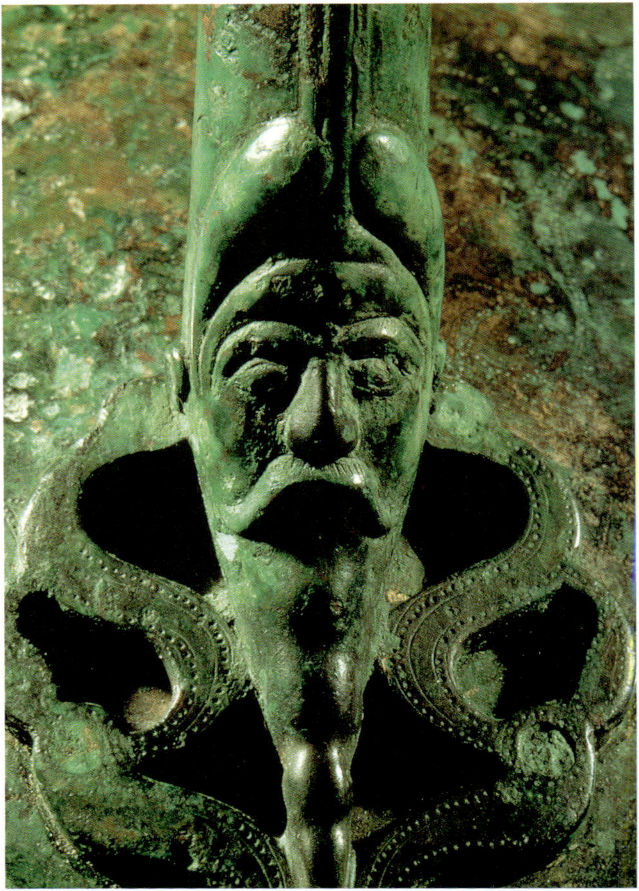

SCULPTURES - BEARDED HEAD JUG HANDLE *left*

4th Century bronze handle on a jug, in the form of a bearded head. Whilst this jug could have been for everyday use, the elaborate decoration of the god-like face suggests that it might have been meant for ceremonial purposes, such as the pouring of libations.

FURTHER READING

The Lindesfarne Gospels; A Masterpiece in Book Painting, Janet Backhouse,The British Library, 1995
The Book of Kells, Bernard Meehan, Thames and Hudson, London 1994.

PICTORIAL ACKNOWLEDGMENTS

All **Gundestrup Cauldron** pieces, National Museum, Copenhagen. **Celtic Helmet,** page 13, Musee des Antiqu. **Human Heads,** pages 14 & 15, Musee Borely, Marseille. **St. John's Gospel,** page 17 & 19, British Library. **St. Mark's Gospel** page 20, British Library. **Bird of Prey,** Musee Borely, Marseille. **Chariot,** Pages 24 & 25, Musee des Antiqu, St. Germain-en-Laye. **Bronze Shield,** page 26 and **Horse's Harness** pages 28 & 29, British Museum, London. **Bronze Jug,** Page 31, Moravska Museum, Brno. **Waterbird Jug,** page 32 & 33, British Museum, London. **Statuette of Horse,** page 35, Landes Museum, Saarbrücken. **Gold Neck Collar,** pages 36 & 37, Staatliches Museum, Saarbrücken. **Celtic Coin,** page 38,Württembergisches Landesmus, Stuttgart. **Plate of Horse's Armour,** page 41, British Museum, London. **Book of Kells,** pages 42, 45 and 46, Trinity College, Dublin. **Human Head Bucket Handle,** page 49, British Museum, London. **Two Severed Heads,** Pages 50 & 51, Musee Granet, Aix-en-Provence. **Bearded Head Jug Handle,** page 52, Rheinisches Landes Museum, Bonn.

All pictures courtesy of AKG London, except all Book of Kells images courtesy of Trinity College Dublin, Beginning of St John's Gospel page 16, Carpet Page cover and page 19, both from the Lindesfarne Gospels, courtesy the British Library. All AKG London images photographed by Erich Lessing, except pages 20, 36 & 37, 38.

OTHER TITLES IN THIS SERIES

PAUL GAUGUIN

CASPAR DAVID FRIEDRICH

ALLEN JONES

SALVADOR DALI

HOKUSAI

PRE-RAPHAELITES

ILLUMINATED MANUSCRIPTS

First published in Great Britain in 1997 by **Brockhampton Press**
20 Bloomsbury Street, London WC1B 3QA
a member of the **Hodder Headline Group**

ISBN 1 86019 483 4
A copy of the CIP data is available from the British Library upon request.

Designed and produced for **Brockhampton Press**
by Keith Pointing Design Consultancy.
Text written by Rowena Smith

Printed and Bound in Italy by L.E.G.O. Spa.